NOTHING LIKE LOVE

Jenny Joseph

NOTHING LIKE
LOVE

ENITHARMON PRESS

ACKNOWLEDGEMENTS

Acknowledgements are due to Bloodaxe Books and Macmillan Children's Books, who published Jenny Joseph's *Selected Poems* (1992) and *All the things I see* (2000), from which several of these poems were taken. Also to *New Statesman*, *Poetry Review*, *The Rialto* and *The Shop*, in which some previously uncollected poems were first printed.

———

Note to 'Nothing like love' on page 48: 'Kathleen' is a reference to the fictional Kathleen of the popular song 'I'll Take You Home Again, Kathleen'. Though this is often thought to be an Irish ballad, it was in fact written by Thomas Westendorf (1848–1923), a music teacher and composer in Plainfield, Illinois, USA.

First published in 2009
by Enitharmon Press
26B Caversham Road
London NW5 2DU

www.enitharmon.co.uk

Distributed in the UK by
Central Books
99 Wallis Road
London E9 5LN

Distributed in the USA and Canada
by Dufour Editions Inc.
PO Box 7, Chester Springs
PA 19425, USA

© Jenny Joseph 2009

ISBN: 978-1-904634-84-3

Enitharmon Press gratefully acknowledges the financial support of
Arts Council England, London.

British Library Cataloguing-in-Publication Data.
A catalogue record for this book is available
from the British Library.

Designed in Albertina by Libanus Press
and printed in England by
Antony Rowe Ltd

CONTENTS

'We only stay alive on what the word means
So why are we frightened of the name of love?'

from 'Language teaching: naming'
in Jenny Joseph's *Rose in the Afternoon*

FANCY FREE

It was the time of daffodils
And I fancy free
So free; as free
As birds that home to nests
Propelled by the season:
And how free are they?

It was the time of the Autumn crocus
And I free, fancy free
Heart so free, as free
As leaves whirling down from trees
Unattached, loosed on the air:
And how free are they?

LADY LOVE

O cat that's licked the cream
A dream
Of satisfaction
A gleam
In the bright eye
That sees over the hedge
Come jump-jump-jumping
Its lady love
Lady Love.

O hat that sits supreme
A-beam
On curly head
That comes up over the hedge
A bob-bob-bobbing
To see love
Lady Love.

To see her as
She rides by
Sparkles in her eye
Laughter in her face
Perfume filling all the space
Where she rides by
Lady Love's cavalcade
Where she rides by
Rides swiftly by
Moving on, going,
Love,
Lady Love
Lady Love
Lady Love.

THE UNLOOKED-FOR SEASON

Love, the sun lies warm along the wall.
The wide windows and the smell of the road
Do not say 'Winter'. Ladybirds are crawling
Out on ledges. Midday full on the land
Slows down the progress of the afternoon
Promising evening, like a summer Sunday.

But look where the sun is. Never high in the sky
It crept around the horizon. Ask anyone,
Look at the trees and the calendar – all declare
It should be Winter. Within two hours
The winter night will come up with the fog.

Since you have come and gone in the dreaded season
And left so much in sunlight, I cannot think
Of now as a dead time, only gentle,
With nothing to be feared, if this is Winter.

CHERRY

Suddenly the cherry has opened.
I could believe it was love
Like the babe opening its eye.

Twig thickening on the air
Has become this burst of blossom.
It waves its appeal in the spring breezes;
O cherry, O open heart.

THE SUN HAS BURST THE SKY

The sun has burst the sky
Because I love you
And the river its banks.

The sea laps the great rocks
Because I love you
And takes no heed of the moon dragging it away
And saying coldly 'Constancy is not for you'.

The blackbird fills the air
Because I love you
With spring and lawns and shadows falling on lawns.

The people walk in the street and laugh
I love you
And far down the river ships sound their hooters
Crazy with joy because I love you.

A CHILD EXPECTING VISITORS

I heard you were coming and
Thrum thrum thrum
Went something in my heart like a
Drum drum drum.

I briskly walked down the
Street street street
To buy lovely food for us to
Eat eat eat.

I cleaned the house and filled it with
Flowers flowers flowers
And asked the sun to drink up the
Showers showers showers

Steadily purring
Thrum, thrum, thrum
Went the drum in my heart because
You'd come, come, come.

BABY'S SONG

Ding-dong   the voices in your head
                the voices in your head
Ding-dong   they fall like gold and lead-
                en voices in your head
Sing-song   the flyers in the sky
                wings cutting through the sky
Sing-song   they lift and then they fly
                the voices in your head
Ping-pong   the balls you puff and pat
                the different games you're good at
Ping-pong   the silly words you say
                to lift the heart, ping-pong.

The sun shoots up the sky
The bird is on the wing
And high high high
Up and down
Rises, falls
Your happy song.

ON THIS BLUE DAY

On this blue day I can't believe
That you
May not be thinking of me. The sun says
It must be true
That you
Are looking up, as I look at this crane
Swinging its giant hook and chain
So gaily
So purposely
So undeniably dangerously
Through
This air
That you
And I
Together breathe;

But as I hold my neck back to gaze
That air shatters
And there are millions of little bits of it,
Like the dust in the sun above the excavations.
I wait to watch will the crane ever come round.
It is afternoon. Miles and miles away you are tiring.

SONG FOR NARCISSUS

I walk in the street and the busman's stare
Makes me feel fat with streaky hair
And I look for Narcissus, who knows I am fair
But he isn't there, he isn't there.

I pass shop windows and am only aware
That a figure I'd rather not know waits there;
I go to a café and sit in a chair
But he's not anywhere, he's not anywhere.

I go back sadly and climb the stair
To my room with no mirror, and hardly a chair
And create at the window, since nobody's there
Narcissus, my own, with a flower in his hair.

HONEY AND GOLD

You will sleep
And you will hear her calling from the lake –
The cool night water-nymph, mind-salving sound –
Sweet as honey, firm as gold.

But no, it will be me longing for your love, me who you do
    not think of,
Walking the restless afternoons in Autumn
When fitfully the town dust swirls and the garbage
Flaps and drifts down streets, streets where no song
But ghetto-blasters blare through the air – me longing for
    your love
That was good as honey, clean as gold!

EURIDYCE

My love has power to force the sea's return
    Up the black rocks, preserve forever its foam;
My love has strength to pull the sun through Heaven
    But not to bring me home.

My love could make the dead cherry-tree stir
    White in the growing grass, had power to give
A paradise to the desert, shyness to the wolf
    But not to make me live.

I HAVE DOUBLED YOUR ROSE

I have doubled your rose
By putting it in water
In a glass I placed
By a looking-glass.

The mirrored flower I put there
Stands for what you gave me:
Illusion of a bloom
Incorruptible.

This rose I picked for you
Has drooped, and now it's fading.
The image pulsing there
Has sunk through layers of glass.

AT THE OPERA

Let us go back, and let me say,
Here as we stand by the wall, this is
The rose I have picked to give to you.

And let me not try not to show
That I mind what you do, that I mind what you say
And that I would travel half England for this.

Let us not always only 'make do'
Digging a ditch for the flood to flow
And siphon the turbulence away.

. . . .

Here I stand by the wall and twist
The rose that I'd brought to give to you.
Thank God I never let you know.

BALLAD OF RODBOROUGH COMMON

High on Rodborough
(*Listen to my tale*)
Stands an empty house
Commanding the vale.

Deep in grass on Rodborough
Two lovers lay
Sleeping murmuring fondling
The hours away.

Heavy in forgetfulness
The man slept;
To her house half down the dell
The woman crept.

Dog rose and elder flower
Pushed gutter high:
A light thrown on her ruined yard
Stopped her cry.

She crawled like a thief to her own back door
Hugging the wall
Two people sat at her table talking:
She heard it all:

He dealt the cards 'What will you lay?'
'I've nothing left but my clothes' she said.
'The clothes from off your back I'll play
Against my holy love,' he said.

He drew and won and had the clothes
As she took them off her back, and then
Fixing his shining eyes on hers
'I'll play you the light from your eyes,' he said.

She drew and gasped. He took her light.
'What else will you give for love?' he said.
'I've nothing left but the skin on my bones,'
'I'll play for the bloom off your skin,' he said.

He drew and laughed and took her skin
And put it away in a box all folded.
'Clothes off your back, light from your eyes, bloom off your skin –
What next?' he said.

The only thing that I've got left
Is what you've had long since,' she said.
'I'll give you the blood that seeps from my womb
To get the other things back,' she said.

He drew and won. He took the blood
'And now I'll have the heart,' he said.
'I'll give you the heart from my body again
If you'll give me yours in exchange,' she said.

'My heart is made of words,' he said
As he dealt the cards for one more spate
'If I give it to you there'll be nothing there
In air it will evaporate.'

He played for her heart and wrenched it out
Of its place in her body 'and now' he said
'What have you left to give for love?'
'There is only the peace of my limbs,' she said.

He took her peace, and anguished and faint
She made a last plea and she drew her last bid
'To get my own love back again
'I'll play you the strings of my mind,' she said.

He played. He won. Got up to go
Leaving her slumped in the chair as dead;
Hand on the kitchen door he turned
Not really listening to what she said.

'Give me a piece of your mind in return
For all the life you've taken,' she said.
'My mind is only a mirror made up
Of pieces out of yours,' he said.

'You have had the joy from my eyes,' she said.
'The bloom from my skin, the skin from my bones
The guts from my belly, the clothes from my back
The peace from my body, my heart from its rest
You have taken all these things and thrown them away.
Are you giving me nothing back?' she said.

'Give me at least my mind again
Which you do not want, which you cannot use
That with it I can grow again
Skin, bloom, light, breath and get once more
All things thereto to make me live.
Give me back my sense again
To see and do the truth,' she said.

'That's not the way the game of love
Is played' he said. 'I did not play
With you' she said, 'and that you know'.
'Of course,' he said 'and that is why
I chose to play the game with you.'

The watching woman found her way
Sick and shaking to the place
They had picnicked and played and slept, and she saw
The man from their house in her lover's face.

The food she had brought him she let fall
And the cover to keep him from the night air
Shaking and sick she went over the hill
That sheltered the man still sleeping there.

Now elder stems grow
Through a broken chair
In a house standing empty
On Rodborough.

THE FEAST

We saw this beautiful confection in the window
Castled and cherried and glazed with dazzling white
Hard as snow crust. Signalled to by delight
We crossed the road. You wanted it for me.

So I, drawing on magic then, planned how, for pleasure
Taking it, I would both have and serve it
For you to eat entire and yet preserve it.
And I went home to summon up a feast.

Then you thought, perhaps it was too much,
Too rich and too bizarre to suit your taste.
And the trimmings on the box were such a waste!
You brought assorted goodies in its stead.

And piled them up into the space I'd made
For the absent astounding centre-piece. Why,
I thought, had I bothered? You kept the ribbon by –
It might come handy for another time.

Having sat and seen the spread all ready
You thought perhaps we'd do without the fruit
On the pudding. It made it difficult to cut.
Absent-minded, you picked at a rim of icing

And turned it round to hide the gap from me.
Then with a flourish set down on a plate
A nice large slice indeed. But I could not eat:
The food looked cardboard-dry and tampered with.

And all the picnic seemed unsavoury:
Bites out of little pies scattered in the sun
Halves of withering sandwiches and everyone
Suddenly with his mind and needs elsewhere.

You moved off fast. You did not stay to clear.
And passing that same window happened to see
(And thought how so much luckier was he)
Who'd got that cake to cut into and swallow
Great luscious mouthfuls, teeth sinking through the icing
(And how you really should have had a share).
You spoilt what was on offer with your care
And self-regard. And so you lost it all.

That magic cake – you could have had it whole.

If you were bred on fairy tales
As was I
You would know where the prince was going to
And why;
And if you had then also lived in the world
As I have done
You would know too that he went past the ten-foot wall of roses
And kept straight on.

And if I told you that somehow he once turned back
And hacked his way through
Would you join in then, and finish the story the way
I wanted you to;
Saying that the clash of light when she woke was
Cymbals of bliss
And the power of life through that long-waiting silence was
All in the kiss;

And agree, since we lounge in the court of a great castle with a
    hundred years' sign
That says: 'For Sale'
It must be that we are bewitched, and that this is
A fairy tale.

ABSTRACT STUDY – CIRCLES

I stand again on the shore
Where we stood and watched the waves.
Or rather, since I write this
I imagine us standing there.

So I sit, town-girt, and imagine
Me standing by you on the shore
But the vision not being a pen
Me writing was only a thought.

I was walking around the streets
Busy, and the mind moving
And now that I sit at my desk
Holding an actual pen
I remember the pleasant morning
When I saw myself sitting down
Late on a warm evening
And fixing this scene of something
That now is so tiny and far
So painted, so set and silent
In the glass of the inner eye

That the only thing left to do
Is to take you by the hand
And run up the bank to the sea
And

I sit here making up that.

X MARKS THE SPOT. A POSTCARD FROM HOME

Lit the fire last night.
Wished you were here;
Stared into the glowing coals;
Thought of you, dear.

Good stretched alone by the fire
Thinking, dear
Nicer things, very likely
Than if you'd been here.

There's the post come.
Nothing from you, dear,
Telling me what you've done
Wishing me there.

Even in the magic fire
Images cool, dear
Come again so I may think that I
Wish you were here.

GETTING BACK HOME

Hang your hat on the peg
Rest up, rest up
Fling your coat on the bed
For you have travelled many miles to see me.

Put your feet on the bench
Rest up, rest up
Heave off your heavy boots
For you have come through winter days to see me.

Settle down by the fire
Rest up, rest up
Lean back and smile at me
For after all this time and travelling
Oh traveller, I'm glad to see you.

BRIDE TO GROOM

For this ring upon my finger
You take the finger.
With the finger you have the hand
And all the winters it was cold as a child;
With the hand you take the arm
And all it has encircled and supported
That now encircles you.
With the arm the shoulder, and the ache in it;
The neck, stiff, and of a stiff-necked people,
And the soft white throat and the hands that have caressed it.

On the neck this head and its thick hair
And under this thick hair the troublous thoughts
The mind that will not let be, nor let you be.
Woven and packed full of twenty-eight years
Which have this day for zenith as one summary.
And with your hand beneath my breast you take
The pumping heart that will not let me be,
And bangs to the sound of traffic, and the ships,
To deaths, arisings, blindness and betrayals
And will not hood the eyes to tell them morning
Is present in the nightmare, or day the dark,
Yet louder than the trumpets says 'I will'
Over the grey and curdling negatives
Rattling before us in the midday sun.
This day we take each other's past and all things
Hateful and marvellous mounting to this moment,
The point of the pyramid on which you slip
This ring to hold
The broad base, and all our future in it.

THE OVERBOLD

Trapeze artists we
Our only net our humanity.
Each hold or leap on which depend our lives
We try now for the first time in the air.
Amateur we improvise where
Only perfected expertise survives.

They say that teeth
Timing, balance or breath
Are not the weaknesses that let you down
But that the beam, travelling from eye to eye,
Like star above a shipwreck holds you high:

Looking in your eyes I drown, I drown.

HERE LIES TREASURE: HERE BE MONSTERS

A child looked in the pool
Where last winter underneath the ice
He'd seen the duck eggs and white pebbles shining.
His eager hand went straight, but, as if blinded
The water clouded and only mud and slime
Grasped his fingers. The pond's grey creature
Swirled in the weed and shivered up his arm.

The mud stirs easily across your face.
The precious stones I surely saw there once
Cloud into useless flint; the guardian monster
Shuts down all access and makes sour the land.

The child would not have nursed his long intent
Had there been nothing there to lure possession.
Without a clay loaded with good perhaps
No jealous spite would bother to be there
And we could dredge the clear but empty water
Or leave the place, since nothing kept us here.

GREAT SUN

Great sun
Eat the clouds up
So that my love can flourish with my garden,
So that my love, my love
And all the busy joy of greenery
Can flourish.

Storm wind
That brings the clouds
Huge and heavy, stifling up the heavens,
Push on, push them over
So that the flattened garden can be righted
And love recover.

CERTAIN WEATHERS

They say love is a great heat.
In these high hot days, then, let us consider the land:
The peony bursts and the sun draws off its colour,
Great unwinking light, morning and evening, lies on
    either hand;
Iron in the sky sucks moisture from under concrete,
Day after day the noon blares 'Here I stand'.

And love, they say, is like a roaring wind
Reversing the grasses; lain low they reveal
Their white uncommon underside; it lashes
The lake's back to an edge scraping a scar in the bank that
    will never heal
The animal rages across the country, it is
A wind, like Orpheus, to make the trees kneel.

Then the tired cooling comes, and in the town
Sapless lies wreckage that the winds brought down.

But no one says that love is changeable
The start-stop rain that has us all in doubt;
A sun enough only to bring out flies;
Wind that pushes our hopes scudding from the horizon, now
    promise now wash-out
Front line forever lost: as finally:
Enemy melted – no victory, no rout.

Underground, stalks fill as the rain seeps in
The earth withstands the drought and hurricane.

MARRIED PEOPLE GOING TO WORK

When I am going on journeys
Drawing through the suburbs in a train
Like one clear thread in a garment of heather tweed,
We seem to be cutting into new territory; new faces
Lap against one's vision, people doing
Different things from us, or at different times.

I have left you, and the little stones I see
Beside the track are not shining in your day.
Of the roadside faces and the clothes the people wear
A window flashing, men stopped for an accident,
The encounters and sights that feed you on your way
I cannot be, for hours, participant.

But the world is round.
The track of love I travel brings me back
To a station where we have been
Where you stand and wait, holding out your hand
All the good of your day on offer
In exchange for all that I have seen.

DAWN WALKERS

Anxious eyes loom down the damp-black streets
Pale staring girls who are walking away hard
From beds where love went wrong or died or turned away,
Treading their misery beneath another day
Stamping to work into another morning.

In all our youths there must have been some time
When the cold dark has stiffened up the wind
But suddenly, like a sail stiffening with wind,
Carried the vessel on, stretching the ropes, glad of it.

But listen to this now: this I saw one morning.
I saw a young man running, for a bus I thought,
Needing to catch it on this murky morning
Dodging the people crowding to work or shopping early.
And all heads stopped and turned to see how he ran
To see would he make it, the beautiful strong young man.
Then I noticed a girl running after, calling out 'John'
He must have left his sandwiches I thought.
But she screamed 'John wait'. He heard her and ran faster,
Using his muscled legs and studded boots.
We knew she'd never reach him. 'Listen to me John.
Only once more' she cried. 'For the last time, John, please wait,
    please listen'.
He gained the corner in a spurt and she
Sobbing and hopping with her red hair loose
(Made way for by the respectful audience)
Followed on after, but not to catch him now.
Only that there was nothing left to do.

The street closed in and went on with its day.
A worn old man standing in the heat from the baker's
Said 'Surely to God the bastard could have waited.'

REDISTRIBUTION

They sat on the polished floor and ate up the huge orange
He had left for his wife.
They got the skin off with his special spring screwdriver
Rusting it, although a fruit knife
Lay in its place in the drawer. On sheets of paper,
Cream linen, kept in a box for the fairest of fair copies
They scribbled little notes and added up,
And used, to unblock a drain
A slender silver pencil he had gone to great trouble to get
Engraved with her name.
Allowing this misuse of her prized possessions
Gave her a sense of freedom – no hoarder she
Of having been fondly thought of in retrospect.
They ripped through the velvet substance he had gathered
With such gloomy care
And walked out guffawing and loving into the sunshine,
        leaving the French windows
To bang and shatter in any storm that came.

'GO BACK TO SQUARE ONE'

We thought we did so well to leave the house
More or less tidy and with no rent owing.
We left the place better than some, we said:
Minimum fuss without disturbing neighbours,
Not enough damage for a landlord's claim
And most of our own baggage still the same.

Surprising, really, how easy in the end
It was to settle down in different towns.
If moving had not muddled up addresses
We would have met to praise ourselves and ask
Why on earth had others made such fuss?
Couldn't they pack up quietly like us?

And then as in the dream when the last step
Brings round the end, only to begin
Without surprise the whole concern again
I found that I was walking past that fence:
Had thought I had packed up and quite cleared out
But only gone a little way about.

I wasn't sure the gas had been turned off
I missed my screwdriver, I'd left some books;
That incompleted letter might be here.
I picked round like a rather stupid thief:
Much worse this time to leave and cross the green
Since I could never tell you I had been.

Then we found we both had business near.
We did not see the house, but now and then
On separate days acknowledged it was there.
We left it well because we never went,
Like blood returning to the famished face
Seemed to forget we'd ever left the place.

REPORTED MISSING

I had a strange dream the other night after I had left you
And it seemed that we were going on a journey.
We had to climb, and a damned difficult climb it was too
In unfamiliar country.

It was rocky, mostly with rivulets, and very bright green patches
And I was always going the long way round
But never got higher, only much further away
From your footsteps' sound.

We were going out of the plains because of your decision
Yet, once above the waterfall, you denied
All thought for the expedition, ignored the ravine
Where the mountain sheep had died.

Suddenly I was in that ravine. Not minding that the ground
Had no real rocks, the clouds neither rain nor snow
I knew that I was lost forever and that
You did not know.

More, that you couldn't care, having gone from the mountain,
        had not forgotten
But being elsewhere would have no cause to remember
That terrible but necessary journey
In a bitter November.

I was quite dead in the darkness for a long time and then I was
        walking down
A bright road that went straight, curved and then went straight
(I can't think why but this was important). I expected
To see you at the gate.

Can habit in dreams work the same as a vision awake? I knew
     you would not
Be there when I arrived, I remembered the climb
My vows on the white road, and yet I expected to see you
The same as the last time.

I can't tell you what it was really like on that climb.
But then it seemed as if – I don't know – it's all different now,
As if you never could have reached my danger,
Never wanted to.

Some dreams one knows for such. Even asleep I knew this
     a dream
Yet when I woke somehow it seemed true.
In sunlight it looks different as I said. I suppose
I shall follow you

On the next climb, get trapped in the same ravine, swear on
     the white road
To endanger nothing again. At any rate
Not my life to one so absent, and again
Look for you at the gate.

THE TORRENT

The torrent blasts through the gorge
Exhilarating, dangerous, beyond death.
Only what is native to this element
Survives in the airless seethe of its champagne.
Its plumey spray explodes at the mile-high wall
And smoke from its rebound fills in the abyss;
It moistens the top of the cliff, greening the lip
Of the dark arid plateau, where some people stand.
They are drawn to look through the boil into the entrails.
Mist swirls and thickens, veiling from the humans
The core of power, knowledge of which is death.

The shaft of a spotlight makes a bright cone of it.
Those at the base looking into its eye
Are held by the luminous point.   Outside,
There's not even nothing. There is no beyond.
The light extinguished or shattered, we are left
Blind on a platform at cliff-edge of dark.
No place that we can know is there, to move to.
And with that néant comes paralysis.
There is no air a human being can breathe.

Keep breathing, though; small movements within that circle
Will push blood through your veins until you can raise
Your eyes to face the blank, and begin to make out,
Where dark thins to a gloom, how, gradually,
Like a dimmer turned up strengthening the light,
Like a blush filling the skin, air permeates.
Evenly, slowly, colour suffuses perspective
Through which a body can move.

Miles from the Falls
Water spills to the plain
And widens over the levels.

Walk out of your house one morning into the town
Into the blue – no mark to fix dimension
As a place to be under. It is just the air.
Scarce visible, comes to your sight by chance
The only wisp in the whole unweighty sky:
Half-moon at Zenith high in the azure stationed.
Curve of nail cuticle strengthens, like a rind hardening,
The infill's diaphanous, a fragment of stippled veil
Transparent threads the wind might move but doesn't.

No personal appointment or passionate need
Has drawn you here, this day like a holiday,
A day that sheds
On nothing very lovely, no Towers of Strength,
On nothing exceptional or desirable –
Benevolence.

A grubby woman heaves herself off the bus and hobbles away.
A well-dressed Jamaican youth turns and approaches: 'Excuse me'.
'Yes?' anxiously; peering. 'Your scarf'. Not hearing: 'My   –   ?'
'You left your scarf on the bus. I picked it up. And then I couldn't
                                                    see you.'
'Oh   thank you. *Thank* you' flinging out hands as if to welcome a child
'It's very special. I'm *so* glad not to have lost it. How very good of you.'
The young one crosses the road, laughingly they gesture their goodbyes
The shafts that beam from their eyes meet through dense traffic,
                                        exchanging pleasure,
Conspiring in love.

The day begins to tire. The shops are crowded.
Two people weave across the road to the chemist
She turning back to shepherd him, whose habit

(Supporting *her*) makes him reach for her elbow.
Thick stockings wrinkle into outsized plimsolls,
His face is large and mottled.   Somehow they get
Into the chemist's. They apologize
To people who block their way; you follow in.
He worries he let the door bang in your face
Turns back to hold it for you now. 'So sorry
To push in front' 'Oh no you didn't' 'Did the door
Hit you? How rude of me!' 'No, not at all' 'I do apologize.'
You want to tell him – but he's ambled off
To find his wife or the things they've come to purchase.

Charisma is not looks or voice or witchcraft.
But a grace of attention, irresistibly attractive,
Affectionate regard, a cherishing.

You want to see them again, to know them a little.

A few pleased words and courtesies to the till girl
Then clutching their packages and each other's hands
Swaying in tandem zig-zag they cross the road.
He turns unsteady at the kerb and in triumph
Thumbs up to the other side, a radiance
Of concern and tenderness and pleasure in it,
And those who see it know it is for them.

The ruinous force, leashed by the gorge it has made,
Thundering through the mountains becomes the great river,
An artery feeding a land where people can live.

LULLABY

Only when we are in each others' arms
Babies or lovers or the very ill
Are we content not to reach over the side;
To lie still,

To stay in the time we've settled in, that we've scooped
Like a gourd of its meat,
And not, like a sampling fly, as soon as landed
Start to our feet,

Pulling one box on another, Ossa on Pelion;
Getting the moment, only to strain away
And look each day for what each next day brings us:
Yet another day;

Pleased with the infant's health and the strength of its
frame
For the child it will grow to,
The house perfected, ready and swept, for the new
Abode we go to,

The town in order and settled down for the night
The sooner for the next day to be over,
The affair pushed straight away to its limit, to leave and
notch up
Another lover.

Lie still, then, babies or lovers or the frail old who
In dreams we carry
Seeking a place of rest beyond the crowds
That claim and harry.
We are trying to reach that island for the festive evening
Where our love will stay –

Waylaid, prevented, we wake as that vivid country
Mists into day.

Stay on this side of the hill.
Sleep in my arms a bit longer.
This driving on will take you over the top
Beyond recall the sooner.

IN HONOUR OF LOVE

In your honour I have cleaned the windows
Of four-months' sorrow-flung obscuration and dirt
And cut my hair and thrown away old rags
That make cupboards foetid, suffused with miserly pain.
I shall wipe the mould out of the corners
Rub down, prepare to paint;   in your honour.

And in your honour
Am throwing out old nastiness with the floorboards,
Memories of hurt, lese-majesty
Along with the shards and glue, useless and hard now.

As if for new love turning a new leaf over
I will pick off infestation up to the minute.
At this time of budding give a chance to cleanliness
Make beds freshly in garden, and in the house
Fresh covers; as if with hope square corners
In expectation, in honour of your coming.

For your comfort and in your honour
I have laid by stores and funds of robustness
Sweeping despondence out with the spiders' coatings
Disinfecting anxiety, self-pity
The damp that clads, sours and eats the woodwork.

I think it isn't true that ghosts return
Only to ruins and to broken things.
Shy visitants that start to come with me
Along the track I make you from the past
By thinking of you, you would never bear
Burdens you could not shoulder when alive.
You'll still want cheering, self-reliance, comfort

The big wheel pulling up the hill, hearth cleared,
Coal ordered, landlord dealt with, 'sociables'.
And so to welcome you and keep a place
For your reviving influence to bide in
I move within the chrysalis of doubt
Wound round for winter comfort, for survival.

In honour of love, in hope of expectation
I leave behind drab covering that kept me
Safe through the winter, safe and solitary.

The grub without its carapace is needed
Pale and soft and vulnerable, for birds
Shining and voracious. So,
I am persuaded, every time a fool.
Well, something must feed the remorselessness of spring.

The skin will burst, so you should see light wings
No dirty brown slough. The bad times swept away,
Place ready for the prodigal,
                                 and be damned the peril
The piercing light and the brief high flight will bring.

Ashes, when you have gone, burnt bits on the lamp
That lit you on your way, but in your honour
As you pass by the window, love – bright flame.

NOTHING LIKE LOVE

Nothing like love, nothing like love Kathleen
For bringing the light up, for seeing and finding it good
For sparking the engine, for feeling it leap into life
And us going with it, turning the world as we go
Oh nothing like love.

And nothing like love, as you know from the songs, Kathleen
Nothing like love for many wasted days;
All the lines dead, all colour blenched from the earth.
For wringing the heart of its blood, for unstringing our gut
No killer like love.

Walk out one morning, arched air one far blue.
Falling in love with the world – true charity.
How large and steady is a life we cherish.
At five or fifty, seventy-eight or three
Nothing like love.